LEARNING TO LOVE YOURSELF

A GUIDE TO SELF-ACCEPTANCE

DR. JAGADEESH PILLAI

Made with ♥ on the Notion Press Platform
www.notionpress.com

|| Dedicated to all wisdom seekers around the world ||

♡♡♡

Contents

Prayer — vii

About The Author — ix

Preface — xiii

1. Understanding Self-love — 1

Part 1

2. The Benefits Of Self-acceptance — 5

Part 2

3. Celebrating Your Triumphs — 9

Part 3

4. Overcoming Self-doubt — 13

Part 4

5. Tackling Negative Thoughts — 17

Part 5

6. Letting Go Of Fear — 21

Part 6

7. Shifting Your Perspective — 25

Part 7

8. Living Mindfully — 29

Part 8

9. Identifying Your Strengths — 33

Part 9

10. Attracting Positive Relationships — 37

Part 10

11. Developing Self-compassion — 41

Contents

Part 11

12. Growing Self-confidence 45

Part 12

13. Nurturing Self-care 49

Part 13

14. Dealing With Emotional Pain 53

Part 14

15. Building Resilience 57

Part 15

Other Books Of The Author 61

Contact 67

Prayer

"Om Bhadram Karnebhih Shrunuyaama
DevaahBhadram Pashyemaakshabhiryajatraah
SthirairangaistushtuvaamsastanoobhihVyashema
Devahitam YadaayuhSwasti Na Indro
VridhashravaahSwasti Nah Pooshaa
VishwavedaahSwasti Nastaarkshyo ArishtanemihSwasti
No Brihaspatir DadhaatuOm Shantih, Shantih, Shantih"

The literal meaning of this mantra is: OM. O Gods! Let us
hear auspicious words from our ears. O reverent Gods! Let
us behold propitious visions from our eyes, let our organs
and body be stable, healthy, and strong. Let us do that
which is pleasing to the gods in the life span allotted to us.
May Indra, inscribed in the scriptures, bring us fortune!
May Pushan, the knower of the world, grant us prosperity!
May Trakshya, who vanquishes enemies, bestow us with
blessings! May Brihaspati bring us success!
OM Peace, Peace, Peace.

༄༄༄

About The Author

Dr. Jagadeesh Pillai is a renowned Guinness World Record holder, writer, and researcher hailing from Varanasi, also known as the abode of Lord Shiva. With a Ph.D. in Vedic Science and a range of creative ideas and achievements, he is a true polymath. He is the author of more than 100 books including Research Publications. Although his roots can be traced back to Kerala, the people of Varanasi hold him in high regard and affectionately consider him one of their own.

In 1998, Dr. Pillai was offered a job at Banaras Hindu University, but he left the position after only two months to pursue greater goals in life. He believed that in order to study Indian scriptures and engage in other creative endeavours, he needed to retire from the daily grind of working solely for money at a young age.

He started an export business from scratch, using the knowledge he had gained from a previous job in the industry. His intelligence and unique approach to business led to great success in a short period of time, earning him more in just a decade and a half than he would have in a lifetime working in a government job. Upon the passing of Dr. APJ Abdul Kalam, Dr. Pillai decided to leave the business and dedicate himself to reading, studying, researching, and experimenting.

During his tenure in the export business, Dr. Pillai traveled to over 16 countries, gaining valuable insight and experiencing the world and life in detail.

Dr. Pillai has achieved four Guinness World Records in the following subjects:

"Script to Screen" - In this record, Dr. Pillai produced and directed an animation film within the shortest time possible, breaking the previous record set by Canadians. He has also received numerous national and international awards and recognitions for this achievement.

Longest Line of Postcards - For this record, Dr. Pillai created a line of 16,300 postcards on the occasion of the 163rd anniversary of Indian Postal Day. The event also included a questionnaire about the Indian flag.

Largest Poster Awareness Campaign - Dr. Pillai designed an awareness campaign on the subject of "Beti Bachao - Beti Padhao" (Save the Girl Child - Educate the Girl Child) to achieve this record.

Largest Envelope - In tribute to the Indian Prime Minister's "Make in India" initiative, Dr. Pillai created a 4000 square meter envelope using waste paper to achieve this record.

Attempted - **70000 Candles on a 210 kg Cake** - To celebrate the 70th Indian Independence Day, Dr. Pillai attempted to light 70,000 candles on a 210 kg cake, which was recorded in World Records India.

Attempted - **Documentary on Dhamek Stupa of Sarnath in 17 Languages** - Dr. Pillai attempted to create a documentary on the Dhamek Stupa of Sarnath, dubbing it in 17 different languages. The result of this attempt is currently awaiting confirmation from the Guinness World Records.

Dr. Pillai is skilled in teaching the Bhagavad Gita, a Hindu scripture, and is popular among young people. He has helped many young people improve their lives through his motivational teachings.

In addition to teaching, he has composed and sung numerous Sanskrit Bhajans and patriotic songs.

He has also written and directed several short films and documentaries for awareness campaigns, and has volunteered with the police in both UP and Kerala to spread awareness about various issues through videos and photography.

Incredibly, he has produced and directed over 100 documentaries about the city of Varanasi, all on his own.

He has also helped and guided more than 25 boys and girls to achieve world records through creative and innovative methods. He is a multifaceted person who uses his intellect and the blessings given to him by God to excel in various areas. He is both a teacher and a student, always learning and teaching, and is able to master any subject he comes across.

He is a selfless social activist and motivational speaker who has overcome struggles and failures to become a successful and enthusiastic individual with a rich life experience.

In addition to his work with the Bhagavad Gita, he is also an efficient Tarot card reader, Astro-Vastu consultant, and a talented singer and composer. He has sung the entire Ram Charita Manas and Bhagavad Gita in his own compositions, and has sung the phrase "Lokah Samastha Sukhino Bhavantu" in 50 different languages. He is currently working on a detailed and scientific study of Vedas, Upanishads, Puranas, and the Bhagavad Gita. He has also composed and sung the Hanuman Chalisa and Gayatri Mantra in 108 and 1008 different compositions, respectively.

Awards - Four Times Guinness World Records, Winner of Mahatma Gandhi Vishwa Shanti Puraskar, Mahatma Gandhi Global Peace Ambassador, Kashi Ratna Award, Dr. APJ Abdul Kalam Motivational Person of the Year 2017, Mother Teresa Award, Indira Gandhi Priyadarshini Award, Bharat Vikas Ratna Award, Udyog Ratna Award, Vigyan Prasar Award, Poorvanchal Ratn Samman.

ঌঌঌ

Preface

Welcome to "Learning to Love Yourself: A Guide to Self-Acceptance". This book was written to help you embark on a journey of self-discovery and growth, as you learn to love and accept yourself for who you are.

Many of us struggle with self-doubt, insecurity, and negative self-talk, making it difficult to feel comfortable and confident in our own skin. We often seek validation from others, instead of finding it within ourselves.

This book aims to provide you with practical tools and insights to help you overcome these challenges and develop a healthier and more loving relationship with yourself. Through a series of chapters and exercises, you will learn to shift your perspective, tackle negative thoughts, and cultivate self-love.

The journey to self-acceptance can be difficult and challenging, but it is also incredibly rewarding. As you learn to love and accept yourself, you will experience greater peace, happiness, and fulfillment in your life.

So, take a deep breath, let go of any expectations and be open to the journey ahead. You deserve to love and accept yourself, and this book is here to guide you on your path.

ᑭᑭᑭ

ONE

Understanding Self-Love

Self-love is a crucial component of self-acceptance and a healthy and fulfilling life. Understanding self-love involves recognizing and appreciating one's own worth, value, and unique qualities, and treating oneself with compassion, kindness, and respect.

Self-love begins with self-awareness. This involves getting to know yourself, your thoughts, feelings, and values, and understanding your strengths and weaknesses. Self-awareness can help you identify areas for growth and improvement and allow you to better understand yourself and your needs.

Another key aspect of self-love is self-compassion. This involves treating yourself with the same kindness and compassion you would offer to a friend. This means being gentle and understanding with yourself when faced with challenges, failures, or setbacks, and recognizing that everyone makes mistakes.

It is also important to engage in self-care practices that nourish and support your physical, emotional, and mental well-being. This can involve exercise, healthy eating, getting enough sleep, and engaging in activities that bring joy and fulfillment. By taking care of yourself, you demonstrate self-love and respect for yourself.

In addition, it is important to surround yourself with positive and supportive relationships. This means seeking out relationships with individuals who encourage, support, and appreciate you, and limiting time with individuals who are negative or draining. By having positive relationships, you can find support and encouragement in your journey towards self-love and self-acceptance.

Finally, it is important to practice positive self-talk. This involves being mindful of the thoughts and beliefs you have about yourself and actively working to shift negative thoughts to positive ones. Positive self-talk can help you cultivate self-love and a healthy self-image.

In conclusion, understanding self-love is an essential aspect of self-acceptance and a fulfilling life. By engaging in self-awareness, self-compassion, self-care practices, surrounding yourself with positive relationships, and practicing positive self-talk, individuals can cultivate a deep sense of self-love and acceptance, leading to a happier, more fulfilling life.

ᑲᑲᑲ

"Your self-worth is not determined by your mistakes; it is determined by how you learn and grow from them."

♡♡♡

TWO

THE BENEFITS OF SELF-ACCEPTANCE

Self-acceptance is a crucial aspect of mental health and overall well-being. By learning to love and accept ourselves, we can experience a range of benefits that positively impact our daily lives.

First and foremost, self-acceptance can lead to improved self-esteem and confidence. By embracing our flaws and imperfections, we can focus on our strengths and the qualities that make us unique. This can help us feel more secure in who we are and increase our overall self-worth.

Additionally, self-acceptance can also help reduce stress and anxiety. By letting go of self-doubt and negative self-talk, we can experience greater peace of mind and a sense of calm.

Another benefit of self-acceptance is improved relationships. When we love and accept ourselves, we are better able to form healthy and meaningful relationships with others. By being more confident and secure in ourselves, we can communicate and connect with others in a more authentic way.

Furthermore, self-acceptance can also lead to increased creativity and productivity. When we let go of self-doubt and negative self-talk, we can free up mental energy and focus on our goals and aspirations. This can help us be more productive and creative in our personal and professional lives.

Finally, self-acceptance can promote overall well-being and happiness. By embracing who we are and accepting ourselves, we can experience greater contentment and joy in life.

In conclusion, self-acceptance has numerous benefits that positively impact our mental health and overall well-being. By learning to love and accept ourselves, we can experience improved self-esteem, reduced stress and anxiety, better relationships, increased creativity and productivity, and greater overall happiness.

ppp

"Your self-worth is not defined by your successes or failures; it is determined by how you view yourself."

ᗪᗪᗪ

THREE

CELEBRATING YOUR TRIUMPHS

Celebrating your triumphs is an important aspect of self-love and self-acceptance. It helps to recognize and acknowledge your achievements, both big and small, and reinforces a positive self-image. Celebrating your triumphs can boost your confidence, increase your motivation, and promote a sense of well-being and joy.

One of the ways to celebrate your triumphs is by keeping a journal or creating a scrapbook of your accomplishments. This can include things like completing a project, learning a new skill, or overcoming a personal challenge. Keeping a record of your triumphs can serve as a reminder of your progress and successes and can help you to stay motivated.

Another way to celebrate your triumphs is to share them with others. Sharing your successes with friends, family, or co-workers can help you to feel valued and appreciated. It can also inspire others and show them the power of perseverance and determination.

Taking time for self-care and indulging in activities that bring you joy can also help you to celebrate your triumphs. This can be as simple as taking a relaxing bath, reading a book, or treating yourself to a special meal. By taking time for self-care, you show yourself love and appreciation and reward yourself for your hard work and achievements.

In addition to celebrating your personal triumphs, it is also important to celebrate the successes of others. Being a supportive and encouraging friend, family member, or co-worker can help to build positive relationships and strengthen your sense of community.

Finally, recognizing and embracing your unique qualities and gifts is an important aspect of celebrating your triumphs. Understanding and accepting your individuality can help you to feel confident and proud of who you are, and lead to a deeper sense of self-love and self-acceptance.

In conclusion, celebrating your triumphs is an essential aspect of self-love and self-acceptance. Keeping a record of your achievements, sharing your successes with others, engaging in self-care, and embracing your individuality can help you to recognize and appreciate your worth, boost your confidence, and promote a sense of well-being and joy.

ϷϷϷ

"Your self-worth is not dependent on the opinions of others; it is determined by your own beliefs and values."

🖤🖤🖤

FOUR

OVERCOMING SELF-DOUBT

Self-doubt can be a pervasive and debilitating experience, affecting every aspect of our lives from our relationships and career to our mental and physical health. However, it is possible to overcome self-doubt and reclaim your confidence.

The first step in overcoming self-doubt is to acknowledge and understand it. Ask yourself where your self-doubt stems from, and try to identify any underlying beliefs or insecurities that are fueling it.

Next, challenge your negative self-talk by questioning the evidence supporting your self-doubt and looking for alternative, more positive perspectives. Reframe negative thoughts with affirmations and positive self-talk.

Surround yourself with supportive people who encourage and believe in you. Seek feedback from trusted friends, family members or mentors, and embrace constructive criticism as a learning opportunity.

Practice self-compassion, treating yourself with kindness and understanding, instead of criticizing and punishing yourself. Give yourself credit for your accomplishments and acknowledge your strengths and positive qualities.

Setting achievable goals and celebrating small victories can help build self-confidence and boost your self-esteem. Engage in activities that you enjoy and make you feel good about yourself.

Finally, be patient and kind to yourself as you work on overcoming self-doubt. Remember, it takes time to change long-standing patterns of negative thinking and behavior, but with dedication and persistence, you can cultivate self-love, acceptance, and confidence.

In conclusion, overcoming self-doubt is a journey, not a destination. By challenging negative thoughts, seeking support, practicing self-compassion, and building self-confidence, you can learn to love and accept yourself, and live an authentic and fulfilling life.

ᗐᗐᗐ

"The greatest act of courage is to be and own
all of who you are."

♡♡♡

FIVE

TACKLING NEGATIVE THOUGHTS

Negative thoughts and self-doubt can be major obstacles in the journey of learning to love yourself. They can prevent us from embracing our authentic selves and accepting our flaws. However, by tackling these negative thoughts, we can learn to love ourselves and cultivate a more positive self-image.

First, it's important to become aware of negative thoughts as they occur. This means paying attention to the thoughts and beliefs that hold you back and learning to challenge them. Rather than automatically accepting negative thoughts as true, ask yourself if they're accurate and if there's evidence to support them.

Next, practice reframing negative thoughts in a more positive light. For example, instead of saying "I'm not good enough," try saying "I am worthy and have unique talents and qualities." This helps build self-confidence and a more positive self-image.

In addition, cultivate a growth mindset and embrace failures and mistakes as opportunities to learn and grow. Let go of perfectionism and the belief that everything must be perfect. Instead, focus on progress and self-improvement.

It's also helpful to engage in self-care and engage in activities that bring you joy and fulfillment. This helps foster a positive outlook and increase overall well-being.

Additionally, seek support from loved ones, friends, or a therapist. Talking to someone about your negative thoughts and receiving encouragement and validation can help you let go of negative self-talk and embrace self-love.

Lastly, mindfulness and meditation can be helpful tools in tackling negative thoughts. By focusing on the present moment and your breath, you can quiet the mind and reduce stress and anxiety.

In conclusion, tackling negative thoughts is a crucial step in learning to love yourself. By becoming aware of negative thoughts, reframing them, embracing failures and mistakes, engaging in self-care, seeking support, and practicing mindfulness and meditation, you can learn to love yourself and cultivate a more positive self-image.

ϸϸϸ

"The greatest act of courage is to be and own
all of who you are."

♡♡♡

SIX

LETTING GO OF FEAR

Fear can be a major roadblock in learning to love yourself. Fear of judgment, failure, and rejection can prevent us from embracing our authentic selves and accepting our imperfections. However, by letting go of fear, we can learn to love ourselves and live a more fulfilling life.

First, it's important to understand that fear is natural and a part of the human experience. Rather than trying to eliminate fear, focus on managing it and allowing it to coexist with your positive emotions and self-love.

Next, identify and acknowledge your fears. Write them down and consider the source of each fear. This can help you gain perspective and see that your fears may not be as valid or limiting as you once thought.

It's also helpful to practice facing your fears. This means taking small steps towards your goals, even if it feels scary or uncertain. By confronting and overcoming your fears, you build self-confidence and resilience, and learn to trust in your own abilities.

In addition, cultivate a growth mindset and embrace failures and mistakes as opportunities to learn and grow. Let go of perfectionism and the belief that everything must be perfect. Instead, focus on progress and self-improvement.

Lastly, seek support from loved ones, friends, or a therapist. Talking to someone about your fears and receiving encouragement and validation can help you let go of fear and embrace self-love.

In conclusion, letting go of fear is a crucial step in learning to love yourself. By acknowledging and managing fear, facing it head-on, embracing failures and mistakes, cultivating a growth mindset, and seeking support, you can build self-confidence and resilience, and learn to love yourself unconditionally.

ϸϸϸ

"Your relationship with yourself sets the tone
for every other relationship you have."

♥♥♥

SEVEN

SHIFTING YOUR PERSPECTIVE

One of the biggest challenges in learning to love yourself is shifting your perspective. Often, we have negative self-talk and limiting beliefs that hold us back from fully embracing and accepting ourselves. However, with a shift in perspective, we can learn to love ourselves, flaws and all.

First, it's important to identify and challenge negative self-talk. This means becoming aware of the thoughts and beliefs that hold us back and learning to reframe them in a more positive light. For example, instead of saying "I'm not good enough," try saying "I am worthy and have unique talents and qualities."

Next, focus on your strengths and accomplishments, no matter how small. Make a list of things you're proud of and things you're grateful for, and regularly remind yourself of them. This helps build self-confidence and a more positive self-image.

It's also important to practice self-compassion. Treat yourself with the same kindness and understanding that you would offer a friend. This means acknowledging and accepting your mistakes, failures, and weaknesses, rather than criticizing or judging yourself.

Additionally, shift your focus from external validation to internal validation. Instead of seeking approval from others, focus on finding happiness and fulfillment within yourself. Embrace your authentic self, rather than trying to fit into someone else's expectations.

Lastly, cultivate gratitude and mindfulness. Take time each day to appreciate the present moment and all that you have in your life. This helps foster a positive outlook and increase overall well-being.

In conclusion, shifting your perspective is a crucial step in learning to love yourself. By challenging negative self-talk, focusing on strengths and accomplishments, practicing self-compassion, embracing authenticity, and cultivating gratitude and mindfulness, you can develop a more positive self-image and increase self-acceptance.

ᐅᐅᐅ

"When one door of happiness closes, another opens, but often we look so long at the closed door that we do not see the one that has been opened for us."

- Helen Keller

♡♡♡

EIGHT
LIVING MINDFULLY

Living mindfully is a crucial aspect of self-love and self-acceptance. It involves being present in the moment, paying attention to your thoughts, feelings, and actions, and being intentional in how you interact with yourself and the world around you. Mindfulness can help to reduce stress, improve mental health, and increase self-awareness, leading to a greater sense of self-love and self-acceptance.

One way to practice mindfulness is through meditation. Meditation can help you to quiet your mind and focus on your breath, allowing you to become more aware of your thoughts and emotions. By regularly practicing meditation, you can develop a more positive relationship with yourself, increase self-awareness, and reduce stress and anxiety.

Another way to live mindfully is through intentional self-reflection. This involves taking time each day to reflect on your thoughts, feelings, and actions, and to identify areas where you can improve. Self-reflection can help you to understand yourself better, become more self-aware, and make positive changes in your life.

It is also important to be mindful in your interactions with others. This includes paying attention to your words and actions, and being intentional in how you treat others. Living mindfully in your relationships can help you to build stronger, more positive connections with others, and lead to a greater sense of self-love and self-acceptance.

In addition, incorporating mindfulness into your daily routines can help you to live in the present moment and reduce stress. This can include simple practices like paying attention to your breathing while doing chores, taking a mindful walk, or focusing on your senses while eating.

Finally, it is important to be kind and compassionate with yourself as you practice mindfulness. Mindfulness is a lifelong journey, and it is important to be patient with yourself and to not judge yourself for any setbacks. Celebrating your progress and being grateful for each moment is a crucial aspect of living mindfully.

In conclusion, living mindfully is a critical aspect of self-love and self-acceptance. Practicing mindfulness through meditation, self-reflection, and intentional interactions with others can help you to become more self-aware, reduce stress, and improve your relationships, leading to a greater sense of self-love and self-acceptance.

ᖡᖡᖡ

"*Learning to love yourself begins with accepting and embracing your imperfections.*"

🖤🖤🖤

NINE

IDENTIFYING YOUR STRENGTHS

Identifying your strengths is a crucial step in the journey towards self-love and self-acceptance. By recognizing and embracing your unique abilities and qualities, you can build a more positive and confident self-image, leading to greater self-love and self-acceptance.

The first step in identifying your strengths is to reflect on your past experiences and accomplishments. Think about times when you felt confident and successful, and consider what qualities or skills may have contributed to these experiences. You can also ask friends, family, and colleagues for their perspectives on your strengths.

Another way to identify your strengths is through personality tests and assessments. There are many online tests and assessments that can help you to identify your personality traits, values, and abilities, providing valuable insights into your strengths.

It is also important to consider your passions and interests when identifying your strengths. These may be hobbies, activities, or subjects that you are deeply interested in and enjoy. Your passions and interests can often reveal your unique strengths and abilities, and can lead you to new opportunities for personal and professional growth.

Once you have identified your strengths, it is important to embrace them and use them to build a positive self-image. This can involve finding ways to incorporate your strengths into your daily life and work, and seeking out opportunities to develop your abilities further.

It is also important to recognize that everyone has weaknesses as well as strengths, and to be kind and compassionate with yourself as you navigate this process. Remember to celebrate your successes and to focus on your strengths, rather than your weaknesses.

In conclusion, identifying your strengths is a critical aspect of self-love and self-acceptance. By embracing your unique abilities and qualities, you can build a more positive self-image and increase your self-love and self-acceptance. Take the time to reflect on your past experiences and accomplishments, consider your passions and interests, and embrace your strengths as you journey towards self-love and self-acceptance.

$$\wp\wp\wp$$

"True self-love is not just about feeling good,
it's about doing what is right for you."

♡♡♡

TEN

ATTRACTING POSITIVE RELATIONSHIPS

One of the most important aspects of learning to love yourself is understanding how your relationships with others are impacted by your self-acceptance. When you have a healthy relationship with yourself, you are better equipped to attract and maintain positive relationships with others.

Self-acceptance helps you set boundaries and communicate your needs effectively, allowing you to attract people who are supportive and understanding of who you are. On the other hand, if you struggle with self-acceptance, you may attract people who take advantage of your lack of confidence or who are not supportive of your growth and well-being.

To attract positive relationships, it is important to focus on building a strong sense of self-worth. This means accepting your flaws, celebrating your strengths, and treating yourself with kindness and compassion. When you have a healthy self-image, you become less likely to tolerate negative or unhealthy relationships and are more likely to attract positive, supportive people into your life.

Additionally, practicing self-care and setting healthy boundaries can help you attract positive relationships. By prioritizing your well-being, you communicate to others that you value yourself and your time, which in turn attracts people who are respectful and supportive of your needs.

Finally, surrounding yourself with positive people and engaging in activities that bring you joy and fulfillment can also help you attract positive relationships. By investing in yourself and your personal growth, you are able to build a supportive network of friends, family, and loved ones who encourage and uplift you.

In conclusion, learning to love yourself is key to attracting positive relationships. By focusing on building self-worth, practicing self-care, and surrounding yourself with supportive people, you can cultivate relationships that bring joy, fulfillment, and happiness into your life. Remember, you deserve to be surrounded by positive, supportive people who love and accept you for who you are.

ᗬᗬᗬ

"Loving yourself is not a destination, it's a
daily practice."

ELEVEN

DEVELOPING SELF-COMPASSION

Developing self-compassion is a key aspect of learning to love and accept ourselves. Self-compassion is defined as treating ourselves with kindness, understanding and empathy, especially in times of difficulty or failure. It involves acknowledging and accepting our own imperfections and struggles, instead of being overly critical and harsh on ourselves.

To develop self-compassion, it's important to start by understanding the difference between self-compassion and self-esteem. While self-esteem involves focusing on our strengths and accomplishments, self-compassion focuses on accepting and embracing our weaknesses and flaws. Self-compassion allows us to extend the same level of understanding and compassion to ourselves that we would offer to a close friend.

One practical way to cultivate self-compassion is to practice mindfulness and self-reflection. By becoming aware of our thoughts and feelings, we can begin to identify negative self-talk and replace it with kind and understanding words. It's also important to challenge self-criticism and remind ourselves that everyone makes mistakes and experiences setbacks.

Another way to develop self-compassion is to engage in self-care activities that promote relaxation and well-being, such as exercise, meditation, and spending time in nature. Taking breaks from stress and overwork can help us to re-energize and refocus, making it easier to approach challenges with a more positive and compassionate attitude.

Finally, it's helpful to seek out supportive relationships and communities, where we can share our struggles and receive encouragement and understanding. Surrounding ourselves with positive and supportive people can help us to feel validated and boost our self-esteem.

In conclusion, developing self-compassion is a crucial step in learning to love and accept ourselves. By embracing our imperfections, taking care of ourselves, and seeking out supportive relationships, we can cultivate a kinder and more compassionate relationship with ourselves, ultimately leading to a more fulfilling and authentic life.

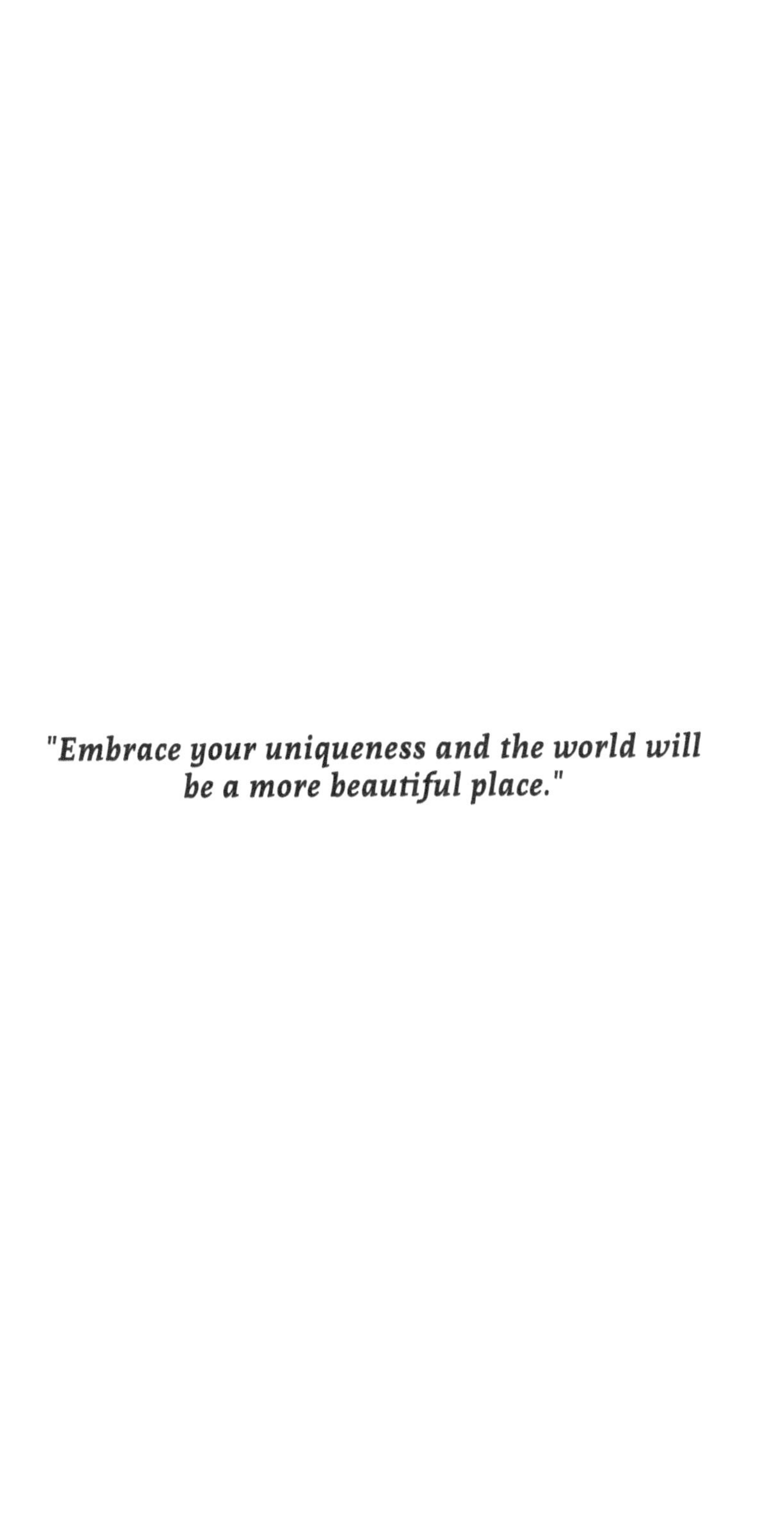
"Embrace your uniqueness and the world will
be a more beautiful place."

TWELVE
GROWING SELF-CONFIDENCE

Growing self-confidence is an important aspect of the journey towards self-love and self-acceptance. Self-confidence is the belief in oneself and one's abilities, and it is a key factor in determining how we feel about ourselves and how we approach life's challenges. Developing self-confidence involves identifying and challenging negative self-talk, setting realistic goals, and taking action to achieve them.

One of the first steps in growing self-confidence is identifying and challenging negative self-talk. This involves recognizing and questioning negative thoughts and beliefs about oneself, and replacing them with positive and empowering thoughts. For example, instead of telling yourself "I can't do this", try telling yourself "I can do this, and I will learn and grow from the experience".

Setting realistic goals and taking action to achieve them is another key aspect of growing self-confidence. This involves breaking down larger goals into smaller, manageable steps, and taking action to move towards those goals. When we set and achieve goals, we build momentum and a sense of accomplishment that can help to boost our self-confidence.

Another important aspect of growing self-confidence is learning to embrace failure and see it as an opportunity to learn and grow. When we view failure as an opportunity to learn and grow, instead of a personal failure, we are less likely to be discouraged and more likely to persevere.

Finally, engaging in self-care activities and taking care of one's physical and mental health is essential for growing self-confidence. This includes engaging in regular physical activity, eating a healthy and balanced diet, getting enough sleep, and taking time to engage in self-reflection and mindfulness practices. By taking care of our physical and mental well-being, we are better able to handle life's challenges and build a foundation of self-confidence that will support us in our journey towards self-love and self-acceptance.

In conclusion, growing self-confidence is an important aspect of the journey towards self-love and self-acceptance. By identifying and challenging negative self-talk, setting realistic goals and taking action to achieve them, embracing failure as an opportunity to learn and grow, and engaging in self-care activities, we can build a foundation of self-confidence that will support us in our journey towards self-love and self-acceptance.

ՔՔՔ

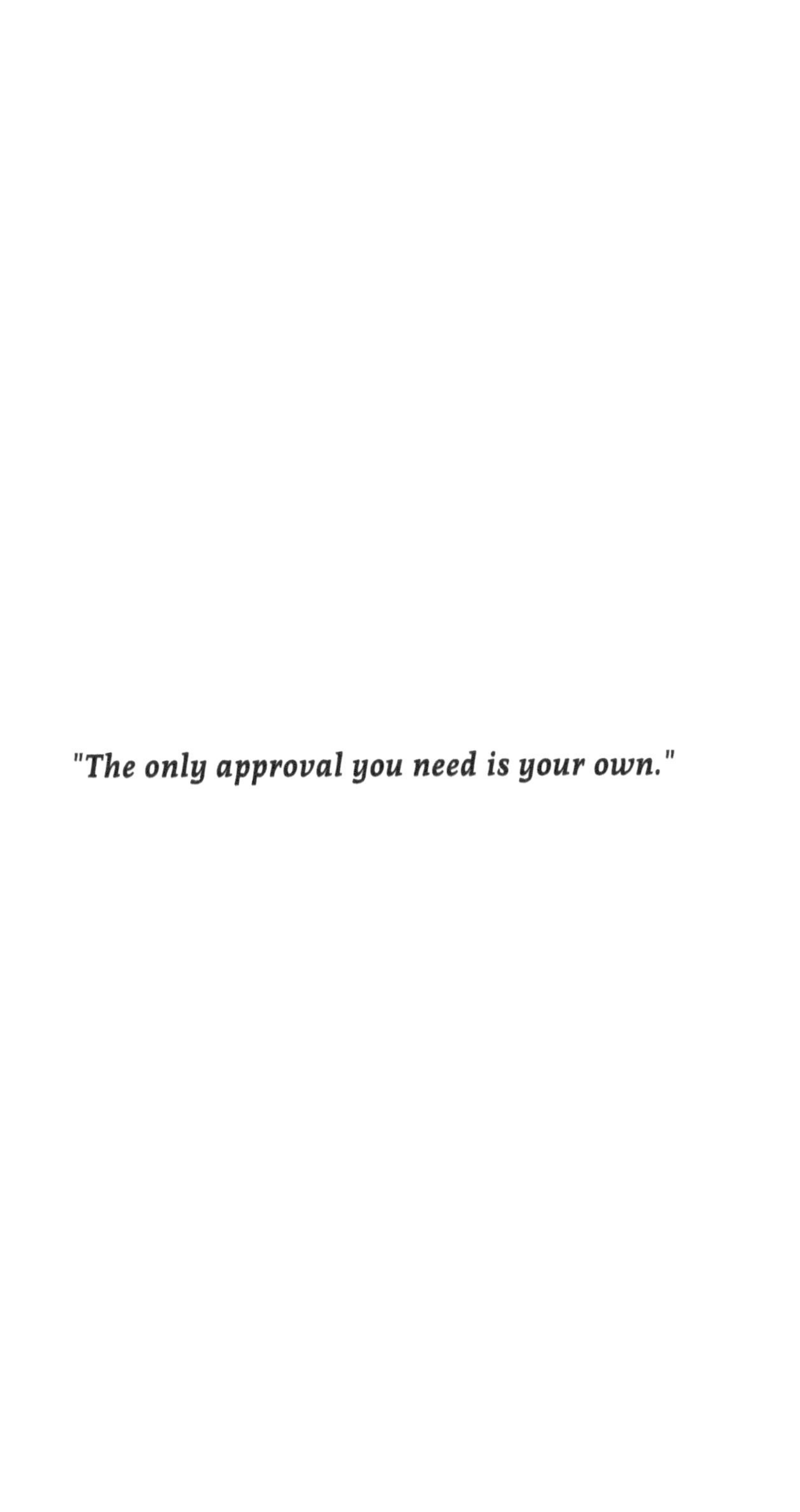
"The only approval you need is your own."

THIRTEEN

NURTURING SELF-CARE

Nurturing self-care is a critical aspect of the journey towards self-love and self-acceptance. Self-care involves taking care of your physical, emotional, and mental well-being through intentional and deliberate actions. By prioritizing self-care, you can build a strong foundation of self-love and self-acceptance, which will support you in your journey towards a more fulfilling life.

One important aspect of self-care is engaging in regular physical activity. This could include anything from yoga and meditation to more intense exercise, such as running or weightlifting. Exercise not only improves physical health but also helps to release endorphins that boost mood and reduce stress.

Another important aspect of self-care is eating a healthy and balanced diet. This means consuming a variety of whole foods, such as fruits, vegetables, and lean proteins, and avoiding foods that are high in sugar, unhealthy fats, and processed ingredients. Eating a healthy diet can improve physical health, boost energy levels, and support emotional well-being.

In addition, self-care also involves engaging in self-reflection and mindfulness practices. This could include journaling, meditation, or other forms of introspection. By taking time to reflect on your thoughts and emotions, you can gain greater insight into your needs, desires, and limitations, and work towards developing greater self-love and self-acceptance.

Finally, it is important to make time for self-care, even when life gets busy. This may involve setting aside dedicated time each day for self-care activities, such as exercise, meditation, or simply relaxing. It may also involve learning to say "no" to obligations and activities that drain your energy and do not align with your values.

In conclusion, nurturing self-care is a critical aspect of the journey towards self-love and self-acceptance. By engaging in physical activity, eating a healthy diet, engaging in self-reflection and mindfulness practices, and making time for self-care, you can build a strong foundation of self-love and self-acceptance that will support you in your journey towards a more fulfilling life.

ꕥꕥꕥ

"Your self-worth is not determined by your successes or failures, but by your inherent value as a human being."

FOURTEEN

DEALING WITH EMOTIONAL PAIN

Dealing with emotional pain is a common challenge in the journey towards self-love and self-acceptance. Emotional pain can arise from a variety of sources, including past experiences, difficult relationships, and personal setbacks. However, it is possible to overcome this pain and find greater self-love and self-acceptance through a variety of strategies and techniques.

One key aspect of dealing with emotional pain is developing a greater understanding of your emotions and the sources of your pain. This may involve exploring your thoughts and feelings through journaling, therapy, or other forms of self-reflection. By gaining a deeper understanding of your emotions, you can begin to identify the root causes of your pain and develop strategies for managing and overcoming it.

Another important aspect of dealing with emotional pain is developing healthy coping strategies. This can involve engaging in self-care activities, such as exercise, mindfulness, or other forms of relaxation. It can also involve seeking support from loved ones, therapy, or other forms of professional help when needed.

It is also important to practice self-compassion and self-forgiveness. This means treating yourself with kindness, empathy, and understanding, even in the face of challenges or setbacks. By embracing self-compassion, you can build resilience, foster greater self-esteem, and reduce feelings of shame and guilt.

In addition, dealing with emotional pain often involves embracing a positive outlook and finding meaning and purpose in your life. This may involve setting achievable goals, developing new interests and hobbies, and engaging in meaningful relationships and activities. By focusing on the positive aspects of your life and finding joy and fulfillment, you can reduce the impact of emotional pain and increase your overall sense of self-love and self-acceptance.

In conclusion, dealing with emotional pain is an important aspect of the journey towards self-love and self-acceptance. By developing a deeper understanding of your emotions, engaging in healthy coping strategies, practicing self-compassion, and embracing a positive outlook, you can overcome emotional pain and find greater self-love and self-acceptance. Remember to take things one day at a time, be kind to yourself, and seek support when needed.

ᑭᑭᑭ

"Loving yourself requires discipline, patience, and an unwavering commitment to your own well-being."

♡♡♡

FIFTEEN

BUILDING RESILIENCE

Building resilience is an important aspect of self-love and self-acceptance. It involves developing the ability to effectively cope with challenges, overcome obstacles, and bounce back from setbacks. This can lead to greater self-confidence, self-esteem, and overall wellbeing, all of which are essential for a healthy and fulfilling life.

One key aspect of building resilience is developing a growth mindset. This involves embracing challenges and setbacks as opportunities for growth and learning, rather than as proof of failure or inadequacy. By cultivating a growth mindset, you can learn from your experiences and develop greater resilience to future challenges.

Another important aspect of building resilience is developing healthy coping strategies. This can involve finding healthy ways to manage stress, such as through exercise, mindfulness, or other forms of self-care. It can also involve seeking support from loved ones, therapy, or other forms of professional help when needed.

Building resilience also involves developing strong relationships and social support networks. Surrounding yourself with positive, supportive individuals can help you to feel valued, accepted, and empowered, even in difficult times. This can include friends, family, or support groups, and can play a critical role in helping you to overcome obstacles and maintain resilience.

In addition to these key strategies, there are many other practical steps you can take to build resilience, such as setting achievable goals, practicing gratitude, and embracing a positive outlook. It is important to find what works best for you and to continuously work on developing your resilience over time.

In conclusion, building resilience is a critical aspect of self-love and self-acceptance. By developing the ability to effectively cope with challenges and setbacks, you can increase your self-confidence, self-esteem, and overall wellbeing, all of which are essential for a healthy and fulfilling life. Take the time to cultivate a growth mindset, develop healthy coping strategies, build strong relationships, and embrace other resilience-building strategies, and you will be well on your way to embracing self-love and self-acceptance.

ᑭᑭᑭ

"The most important relationship in your life
is the one you have with yourself."

♡♡♡

Other Books Of The Author

1. The Moments When I Met God
2. Kashiyile Theertha Pathangal
3. GURU GYAN VANI
4. Abhiprerak Gita
5. ASSI SE JAIN GHAT TAK
6. Hopelessness of Arjuna
7. The Soul and It's True Nature
8. Sense of Action (Karma)
9. Action through Wisdom
10. Action through Wisdom
11. THEORY AND PRACTICAL OF EVERY ACTION
12. LOGICAL UNDERSTANDING OF THE SUPREME
13. THE IMPERISHABLE SUPREME
14. Yatra Nishadraj se Hanuman Ghat Tak
15. Yatra Karnatak Ghat se Raja Ghat Tak
16. Yatra Pandey Ghat se Prayagraj Ghat Tak
17. Yatra Ranjendra Prasad Ghat se Dattatreya Ghat Tak
18. YaatraSindhiya Ghat se Gwaliar Ghat Tak
19. Yatra Mangala Gauri Ghat se Hanuman Gadhi Ghat Tak
20. Yatra Gaay Ghat Se Nishad Ghat Tak
21. MAA GANGA, GHATEN EVM UTSAV
22. Ganga Arti Dev Deepavali evam Any Utsav
23. Potentials of Digitalized India
24. VEDIC CONSCIOUSNESS
25. A Brief Introduction to Vedic Science
26. Kashi ke Barah Jyotirling
27. IMPACT OF MOTIVATION
28. Let's have a Milky Way Journey
29. Color Therapy in a Nutshell

30. Rigveda in a Nutshell
31. Yajurveda in a Nutshell
32. Samveda in a Nutshell
33. Atharva Veda in a Nutshell
34. Ayushman Bhava - Ayurveda
35. Srimad Bhagavad Gita and Upanishad Connection
36. Srimad Bhagavad Gita - an attempt to summarize each chapter.
37. Facts and Impact of Nakshatra
38. Astro Gems - NAVARATNA
39. Ekadashi - A Concise Overview
40. A Concise View of Hanuman Chalisa
41. Inspirational Gita
42. Nakshatraranyam
43. Summary of 18 Mahapuranas
44. Synopsis of 18 Upa Puranas
45. Rigvediya Upanishads
46. Shukla Yajurvediya Upanishads
47. Krishna Yajurvediya Upanishads
48. Samavediya Upanishads
49. Atharvavediya Upanishads
50. The Seven Great Sages
51. From Rocket Scientist to President Dr. APJ Abdul Kalam
52. The Visionary's Voice - Quotes of Dr. APJ Abdul Kalam
53. The Wisdom of Swami Vivekananda: Insights and Inspiration from a Legendary Spiritual Teacher
54. Ayurvedic Remedies from the Garden
55. Sages and Seers
56. Rising Strong – Motivational Stories of Women
57. Beyond Flames -Mystery stories of Funeral Ghat Manikarnika
58. The Origins of Tulsi: A Look at the Mythological Roots of the Plant"

59. The Holistic Cow: A Look at the Physical, Spiritual, and Cultural Importance of Cows in India
60. Arts of Healing
61. Exploring the Divine
62. Understanding Five Elements
63. The Etymology of Ram
64. Symbols of India
65. Voice of Change (About Speeches of Great Men)
66. She Speaks (About Speeches of Great Women)
67. Patriotism on Celluloid – Brief About Patriotic Films
68. The Music of Motivation: A Brief Guide to Inspirational Film Songs
69. **Unlocking the Secrets of the Dashopanishads**
70. A Cultural Mosaic
71. Ancient Traditions, Modern Minds
72. Ecos of Ancient Wisdom
73. Beneath the Surface
74. From Temples to Ashrams
75. Sages of the Subcontinent
76. The Art of Healling (Ayurveda, Yoga & Naturopathy)
77. Indian Kitchen
78. The Festivals of India
79. The Indian Epics Retold
80. The Power of Mantras
81. The Indian River Ganges
82. The Indian Architecture
83. Rites of Passage
84. The Indian Silk Road
85. The Indian Literature
86. The Indian Villages
87. The Indian Folks & Crafts
88. The Way of Buddha
89. The Ramayan of Tulsidas

90. Astrological Remedies
91. The Secret Power of Motivation
92. Secret of Developing your Inner Strength
93. The Secret Path to Motivation
94. The Art and Secret of Positive Thinking
95. The Secrets of Practicing Ethical Living
96. Indian Art and Painting
97. The Indian Herbalism
98. Bharatanatyam to Kathak
99. Exploring India's Astrological Remedies
100. The Indian Festival of Flowers
101. Indian Handicrafts
102. The Splashes of Joy – India's Colour Festival
103. The Indian Science of Astrology
104. The Indian Mythology
105. Path to Enlightenment
106. The Indian Spirituality for Children
107. Aromas of India
108. The Secrets of Healthy Relationships
109. Ancestral Ties
110. The Indian Street Food
111. Discovering America
112. The Indian Textile
113. Listening to Motivational Speeches
114. Taste of India
115. A Cultural Journey through Indian Nuptials
116. Motivational Quote for Change
117. Secret Strategies for Making Money
118. Secrets to Cultivate a Positive Mindset
119. A Tapestry of Cultures: Exploring India from Kashmir to Kanyakumari
120. Achieving Your Dreams with Resilience: Secret Strategies for Overcoming Obstacles

121. Innovative Startups - 25 Startup Ideas to Spark Your Business Creativity
122. Export Management: Strategies for Global Success
123. Exporting from India - A Step by Step Guide
124. Finance Fundamentals: Mastering Financial Management for Business Success
125. Global Growth Strategies for International Business Development
126. Marketing Mastery: Unlocking the Secrets of Modern Marketing
127. Operations Mastery: Managing the Flow of Value in Business
128. Strategic Business Management: Navigating the Modern Business Landscape
129. Human Resource Management Strategies for Building and Managing a High Performance Team
130. The Indian Landscapes and Nature: An Exploration Of India's Natural Beauty And Diversity
131. The Indian Street Performances: A Cultural Exploration of India's Street Performances
132. Affirming Your Self-Worth: Strategies for Achieving Emotional Wellbeing
133. Cultivating Self-Discipline: Secrets Methods for Achieving Your Goals
134. Embracing Change: Strategies for Adapting to Life's Challenges
135. Embracing Your Uniqueness: Secret Strategies for Living an Authentic Life
136. Finding Motivation in Despondency: Coping with Difficult Times

ppp

Contact

DR. JAGADEESH PILLAI

MBA & PhD in Vedic Science

Four Times Guinness World Record Holder

Winner of Mahatma Gandhi Vishwa Shanti Puraskar and
Global Peace Ambassador

Gemology, Astro & Vastu Consultant - Spiritual Counselor

Consultant for designing World Record Ideas

Efficient Tarot Card Reader

9839093003

myrichindia@gmail.com

drjagadeeshpillai@facebook

drjagadeeshpillai@instagram
jagadeeshpillai@youtube

www. JAGADEESHPILLAI.com

❧❧❧

|| LOKAHA SAMASTHAHA SUKHINO BHAVANTU ||

ᘐᘐᘐ